EXECUTIVE FUNCTIONING SKILLS FOR STUDENTS WITH AUTISM

A practical guide to helping students with autism master planning, organization, time management, and more

CELESTIA EMBER

Copyright © 2024 by Celestia Ember

All rights reserved. No part of this book may be reproduced or transmitted in any form or by any means, electronic or mechanical, including photocopying, recording, or by any information storage and retrieval system, without permission in writing from the publisher.

The information provided in this book is designed to provide helpful information on the subjects discussed. The author and publisher disclaim any liability or loss in connection with the use or misuse of this information. It is recommended that readers consult with appropriate professionals before taking any actions based on the information in this book.

TABLE OF CONTENTS

CHAPTER 1 15
UNDERSTANDING AUTISM AND EXECUTIVE FUNCTIONING 15
What is Autism Spectrum Disorder? 16
Defining Executive Functioning 19
How Autism Affects Executive Functioning 23
Common Challenges and Strengths 27

CHAPTER 2 31
ASSESSMENT AND EVALUATION OF EXECUTIVE FUNCTIONING 31
Assessment Tools and Techniques 32
Collaborating with Professionals for Comprehensive Evaluation 36
Ethical Consideration and Challenges 39

CHAPTER 3 45
STRATEGIES FOR BUILDING EXECUTIVE FUNCTIONING SKILLS 45
Creating a Supportive Environment 46

Establishing Routines and Structures 50

Visual Supports and Schedules 55

Teaching Self-Monitoring and Self-Regulation Techniques 60

CHAPTER 4 65

ENHANCING PLANNING AND ORGANIZATION SKILLS 65

Breaking Tasks into Manageable Steps 66

Using Task Lists and Checklists 69

Organizational Systems and Tools 73

CHAPTER 5 79

DEVELOPING TIME MANAGEMENT SKILLS 79

Understanding the Concept of Time 80

Teaching Time Management Strategies 84

Using Timers and Alarms Effectively 88

CHAPTER 6 93

IMPROVING FLEXIBILITY AND ADAPTABILITY 93

Understanding Rigidity and Flexibility in Autism 94

Strategies for Teaching Flexibility 99

Chapter 7 105

WORKING WITH PARENTS AND CAREGIVERS 105

Building Partnerships with Families 106

Providing Resources and Support for Parents 107

Collaborating on Strategies for Home and School 108

Conclusion 110

Every individual with autism is a unique masterpiece, deserving of understanding, acceptance, and unwavering support on their journey.

INTRODUCTION

Executive functioning (EF) refers to a set of cognitive processes crucial for managing and regulating various aspects of behavior and cognition. These processes include but are not limited to planning, organization, time management, problem-solving, cognitive flexibility, and impulse control. Essentially, EF acts as the "command center" of the brain, facilitating goal-directed behavior and adaptive functioning across different contexts.

Students diagnosed with Autism Spectrum Disorder (ASD) often encounter specific challenges related to EF skills. ASD is characterized by neurodevelopmental differences that can impact the typical development and utilization of EF abilities. Individuals with ASD may struggle with planning and organizing tasks, maintaining attention and focus, transitioning between activities, and adapting to changes in routines or environments. These difficulties can significantly affect their academic performance, daily functioning, and social interactions.

Research suggests a high prevalence of EF difficulties among individuals with ASD, with estimates indicating that up to 80% may experience challenges in this domain. The underlying reasons for these difficulties are complex and multifaceted, reflecting the intricate interplay of genetic, neurobiological, and environmental factors. Differences in brain connectivity, neurotransmitter function, and executive control networks are among the potential contributors to EF impairments in ASD.

The impact of EF deficits extends beyond academic settings, influencing various aspects of individuals' lives. In educational settings, students with ASD may struggle to complete assignments, follow instructions, or organize their materials, leading to academic underachievement or difficulties with classroom behavior. In daily life, challenges with EF can manifest in difficulties managing personal tasks, maintaining routines, or adhering to schedules. Moreover, deficits in EF skills can affect social interactions, as individuals with ASD may find it challenging to navigate social nuances, understand others' perspectives, or regulate their behavior in social contexts.

Developing strong executive functioning (EF) skills is paramount for students with Autism Spectrum Disorder

(ASD) to thrive across multiple domains of their lives. EF skills serve as the foundation for effective goal-setting, problem-solving, and self-regulation, enabling individuals to navigate the complexities of academic, social, and personal challenges with greater ease and success.

First and foremost, strong EF skills are instrumental in academic achievement for students with ASD. Consider the task of completing homework assignments. Students with well-developed EF skills can efficiently plan out their tasks, organize their materials, and manage their time effectively to meet deadlines. They can break down complex assignments into manageable steps, prioritize tasks based on importance, and maintain focus amidst distractions. As a result, they are better equipped to excel academically, demonstrating improved performance on tests and assignments. Moreover, proficient EF skills facilitate learning comprehension and retention, as students can engage in critical thinking, problem-solving, and information processing with greater efficiency.

Beyond academics, EF skills play a crucial role in facilitating successful social interactions for individuals with ASD. Social situations often require flexibility, perspective-taking, and impulse control – all of which are components of EF. For instance, imagine a group conversation where participants take turns speaking and responding to each other's ideas. Students with strong EF skills can regulate their impulses to interject, actively listen to others, and formulate appropriate responses based on social cues. They can also adapt their communication style and behavior to fit different social contexts, fostering meaningful connections and friendships. Additionally, proficient EF skills enable individuals to navigate social nuances, resolve conflicts, and collaborate effectively in group settings, enhancing their overall social competence and peer relationships.

In terms of independent living, EF skills are essential for managing everyday tasks and responsibilities autonomously. From planning meals and grocery shopping to organizing personal belongings and maintaining a tidy living space, individuals with strong EF skills can effectively manage the demands of daily life. For example, they can create shopping lists, adhere to budgets, and follow recipes to prepare meals independently. They can also establish routines and schedules to ensure timely completion of chores and self-care activities.

Moreover, nurturing EF skills has long-term benefits for individuals with ASD, extending beyond immediate academic and social contexts. As individuals develop proficiency in EF skills, they gain valuable tools for adapting to new situations, managing stress, and regulating their emotions. For instance, imagine a job interview where unexpected questions are posed. Individuals with strong EF skills can remain composed under pressure, organize their thoughts coherently, and respond thoughtfully to the interviewer's inquiries. Additionally, proficient EF skills enable individuals to set realistic goals, devise action plans, and monitor their progress towards achieving desired outcomes. As a result, they experience increased self-confidence, resilience, and adaptability in navigating life's challenges.

Furthermore, strengthening EF skills empowers individuals with ASD to pursue their aspirations and aspirations with greater autonomy and agency. Whether it's pursuing higher education, pursuing a career, or engaging in leisure activities, individuals with well-developed EF skills can overcome barriers and seize opportunities for personal growth and fulfillment. For instance, imagine a student with ASD who dreams of attending college. With strong EF skills, they can navigate the college application process, manage their academic workload, and advocate for their needs and accommodations effectively. Similarly, in the workplace, individuals with proficient EF skills can excel in various roles, demonstrating initiative, problem-solving abilities, and teamwork skills that contribute to their professional success.

Overview of the Book

This book will serve as a comprehensive guide for parents, educators, therapists, and other professionals working with individuals on the autism spectrum. Through a practical and compassionate approach, this resource aims to support the development of essential executive functioning (EF) skills in students with ASD, empowering them to succeed academically, socially, and personally.

This book will begin with an introduction to the concept of executive functioning and its significance in the lives of individuals with ASD. It will delve into the specific challenges faced by these students in developing and utilizing EF skills, highlighting the impact on academic performance, daily functioning, and social interactions. Moreover, the book will address the prevalence of EF difficulties in individuals with ASD and explore potential underlying reasons for these challenges.

Subsequent chapters will focus on strategies and interventions to enhance key areas of EF skills. These include planning and organization, time management, flexibility and adaptability, problem-solving and decision-making, and social skills and collaboration. Each chapter will provide practical tips, evidence-based practices, and real-life examples to illustrate how EF skills can be nurtured and applied in various contexts.

For instance, in the chapter on planning and organization, this book will offer strategies for breaking tasks into manageable steps, using visual supports and schedules, and establishing routines and structures. These strategies are designed to help students with ASD effectively plan their activities, manage their materials, and stay organized, thereby improving their academic performance and reducing stress.

Similarly, the chapter on time management will explore techniques for teaching the concept of time, using timers and alarms effectively, and creating schedules to structure daily routines. By developing these skills, students with ASD can learn to allocate their time efficiently, prioritize tasks, and meet deadlines, leading to greater independence and self-confidence.

Furthermore, this book will address the importance of fostering flexibility and adaptability in students with ASD, providing strategies for coping with changes and transitions, teaching social problem-solving, and promoting collaborative skills. These skills are essential for navigating the complexities of social interactions, adapting to new situations, and thriving in diverse environments.

Throughout the book, the overarching goal will be to empower readers with practical tools and strategies to support the development of EF skills in students with ASD. By adopting an evidence-based and compassionate approach, this resource will aim to equip parents, educators, therapists, and other professionals with the knowledge and resources needed to foster success and well-being in individuals on the autism spectrum.

CHAPTER 1

UNDERSTANDING AUTISM AND EXECUTIVE FUNCTIONING

WHAT IS AUTISM SPECTRUM DISORDER?

Autism Spectrum Disorder (ASD) is a neurodevelopmental condition characterized by persistent challenges in social communication and interaction, as well as restricted, repetitive patterns of behavior, interests, or activities. It is considered a "spectrum" disorder because it encompasses a wide range of symptoms, severity levels, and associated features that vary from person to person. While individuals with ASD share certain commonalities, such as difficulties with social interaction and repetitive behaviors, the manifestation and severity of these features can differ significantly among individuals, leading to the term "spectrum."

At the core of ASD are impairments in social communication and interaction. This may manifest as difficulties in understanding and using nonverbal cues such as eye contact, facial expressions, and gestures. Individuals with ASD may struggle with initiating and maintaining conversations, interpreting others' emotions and intentions, and developing and maintaining friendships. Additionally, they may exhibit challenges in understanding and adhering to social norms and conventions.

Another hallmark of ASD is the presence of restricted, repetitive patterns of behavior, interests, or activities. This may include repetitive movements or speech (e.g., hand-flapping, echolalia), adherence to rigid routines or rituals, intense preoccupation with specific interests or topics, and sensory sensitivities or aversions. These repetitive behaviors and restricted interests often play a central role in the lives of individuals with ASD and may serve as coping mechanisms or sources of comfort.

The diagnostic criteria for ASD are outlined in the Diagnostic and Statistical Manual of Mental Disorders, Fifth Edition (DSM-5), published by the American Psychiatric Association. To receive a diagnosis of ASD, an individual must demonstrate persistent deficits in social communication and interaction, as well as restricted, repetitive patterns of behavior, interests, or activities, across multiple contexts. These symptoms must be present during early childhood, typically before the age of three, and significantly impact the individual's functioning and daily life.

It is essential to seek professional evaluation for ASD if there are concerns about a child's development or behavior. Early identification and intervention can lead to improved outcomes and better support for individuals with ASD and their families. A comprehensive evaluation typically involves assessments conducted by a multidisciplinary team, which may include psychologists, pediatricians, speech-language pathologists, and other specialists. The evaluation process may include interviews with caregivers, direct observation of the individual's behavior, standardized assessments, and developmental screenings.

The prevalence of ASD has increased in recent years, with estimates suggesting that approximately 1 in 54 children in the United States have been diagnosed with ASD. Importantly, ASD affects individuals across all genders, ethnicities, and socioeconomic backgrounds, highlighting the importance of awareness, understanding, and support for individuals with ASD and their families.

While ASD is a lifelong condition, early intervention and ongoing support can make a significant difference in the lives of individuals with ASD. Evidence-based interventions, such as applied behavior analysis (ABA), speech and language therapy, occupational therapy, and social skills training, can help individuals with ASD develop essential skills, improve communication and social interaction, and enhance their overall quality of life. Additionally, accommodations and supports in educational, vocational, and community settings can facilitate inclusion and promote success for individuals with ASD across the lifespan.

DEFINING EXECUTIVE FUNCTIONING

Executive functioning (EF) is like the conductor of an orchestra, coordinating and directing all the different instruments to create a harmonious and well-organized performance. In the orchestra of our minds, EF serves as the conductor, guiding our thoughts, actions, and behaviors to help us achieve our goals and navigate the complexities of daily life.

At its core, executive functioning encompasses a set of mental skills that enable us to plan, organize, manage time, remember information, and regulate our emotions and behaviors. These skills are essential for completing tasks, solving problems, making decisions, and adapting to changing situations effectively. Think of executive functioning as the CEO of our brain, overseeing and coordinating various cognitive processes to ensure optimal performance.

One of the key components of executive functioning is planning. Planning involves setting goals, breaking them down into smaller steps, and creating a roadmap to achieve them. For example, when planning a vacation, we need to decide on a destination, research travel options, book accommodations, and create an itinerary. Without effective planning skills, we may struggle to organize our trip and may encounter difficulties along the way.

Organization is another critical aspect of executive functioning. Organization entails arranging and structuring information, materials, and tasks in a systematic and orderly manner. This may involve keeping track of appointments, maintaining a tidy workspace, and categorizing documents or belongings. Organizational skills help us stay on top of our responsibilities and prevent things from slipping through the cracks.

Time management is also an essential component of executive functioning. Time management involves prioritizing tasks, allocating time effectively, and meeting deadlines. It requires us to balance competing demands and make efficient use of our time. Effective time management allows us to accomplish more in less time and reduces stress and procrastination.

Working memory is another key aspect of executive functioning. Working memory refers to our ability to hold and manipulate information in our mind over short periods. It allows us to follow instructions, solve problems, and engage in complex tasks. For example, when following a recipe, we need to remember the ingredients, their quantities, and the steps involved in the cooking process. Working memory enables us to retain this information and execute the task successfully.

Self-control, or impulse control, is another crucial component of executive functioning. Self-control involves regulating our thoughts, emotions, and behaviors to resist immediate temptations and achieve long-term goals. It requires us to manage impulses, delay gratification, and exercise restraint in challenging situations. For instance, resisting the urge to eat a piece of cake when trying to stick to a healthy eating plan requires self-control.

The prefrontal cortex, located at the front of the brain, plays a central role in supporting executive functioning. Often referred to as the brain's "CEO," the prefrontal cortex is responsible for higher-order cognitive functions, including decision-making, problem-solving, and impulse control. It acts as the command center for executive functioning, coordinating activities across different brain regions to facilitate goal-directed behavior and adaptive functioning.

Executive functioning skills are essential for individuals of all ages and abilities. From managing household chores and balancing budgets to succeeding in school and advancing in careers, executive functioning skills play a vital role in everyday life. Moreover, executive functioning skills are particularly crucial for individuals with neurodevelopmental disorders, such as ADHD or autism spectrum disorder, who may experience challenges in these areas.

HOW AUTISM AFFECTS EXECUTIVE FUNCTIONING

Autism Spectrum Disorder (ASD) is a complex neurodevelopmental condition that can profoundly affect the development and utilization of executive functioning (EF) skills. EF skills, which encompass a range of cognitive processes involved in planning, organization, time management, working memory, and self-regulation, are essential for navigating the demands of daily life. However, individuals with ASD often experience challenges in these areas, which can impact their ability to function effectively in various contexts.

One way in which ASD affects executive functioning is through social communication challenges. Individuals with ASD may struggle to understand and interpret social cues, such as facial expressions, tone of voice, and body language. This difficulty in understanding social cues can hinder their ability to engage in effective communication and form meaningful relationships. For example, a child with ASD may have difficulty initiating conversations, maintaining eye contact, or understanding the perspectives of others, all of which are important aspects of social interaction that rely on executive functioning skills.

Furthermore, sensory processing differences commonly observed in individuals with ASD can also contribute to difficulties with executive functioning. Many individuals with ASD experience heightened sensitivity or aversion to sensory stimuli, such as loud noises, bright lights, or certain textures. These sensory sensitivities can be overwhelming and distracting, making it challenging for individuals to focus, concentrate, or regulate their attention effectively. As a result, tasks that require sustained attention or concentration may be particularly difficult for individuals with ASD, impacting their ability to engage in activities that require strong EF skills.

Moreover, the presence of restricted interests and repetitive behaviors, which are characteristic features of ASD, can further impact executive functioning. Individuals with ASD may become intensely focused on specific topics or activities, to the exclusion of other tasks or responsibilities. This hyper-focus on particular interests can interfere with their ability to shift attention, prioritize tasks, or adapt to changing demands. For example, a child with ASD may become so engrossed in a particular topic or activity that they have difficulty transitioning to other activities or completing tasks that are unrelated to their interests.

Research has consistently shown a link between ASD and difficulties with executive functioning. Studies have found that individuals with ASD tend to exhibit deficits in various EF skills, including planning, organization, working memory, and cognitive flexibility. For example, a meta-analysis conducted by Leung and colleagues (2015) found that individuals with ASD demonstrated impairments in planning and organization, as well as difficulties with cognitive flexibility and inhibitory control, compared to typically developing individuals. These findings highlight the pervasive nature of EF difficulties in individuals with ASD and underscore the importance of addressing these challenges in intervention and support programs.

In daily life, the impact of executive functioning difficulties on individuals with ASD can be profound. For children with ASD, difficulties with planning and organization may manifest as challenges in completing homework assignments, following classroom routines, or managing their belongings. For adults with ASD, difficulties with time management and self-regulation may affect their ability to maintain employment, manage household responsibilities, or engage in social activities. Moreover, executive functioning difficulties can contribute to feelings of frustration, anxiety, or low self-esteem in individuals with ASD, as they may struggle to meet the expectations of others or achieve their own personal goals.

Despite the challenges associated with ASD and executive functioning, there are strategies and interventions that can help support individuals in developing and strengthening these skills. For example, visual supports, such as visual schedules or checklists, can help individuals with ASD organize their tasks and manage their time more effectively. Additionally, behavioral strategies, such as breaking tasks into smaller steps or providing clear and consistent instructions, can help individuals with ASD overcome difficulties with planning and organization. Occupational therapy and sensory integration techniques can also be beneficial for addressing sensory sensitivities and improving attention and focus.

COMMON CHALLENGES AND STRENGTHS

Individuals with Autism Spectrum Disorder (ASD) often face a variety of challenges related to executive functioning (EF) skills, which can impact their ability to navigate daily life effectively. Understanding these common challenges is essential for providing targeted support and intervention to individuals with ASD. Additionally, it's important to recognize that individuals with ASD also possess unique strengths that can be leveraged to support the development of EF skills.

One of the most common EF challenges faced by individuals with ASD is difficulties with organization. Organizational skills involve arranging and structuring information, materials, and tasks in a systematic and orderly manner. Individuals with ASD may struggle to keep track of their belongings, maintain a tidy workspace, or follow through with routines and schedules. For example, a child with ASD may have difficulty organizing their school supplies or keeping their bedroom neat and organized. This can lead to difficulties in finding important items, completing tasks on time, and maintaining consistency in daily routines.

Planning is another area of executive functioning that can pose challenges for individuals with ASD. Planning skills involve setting goals, breaking them down into smaller steps, and creating a roadmap to achieve them. Individuals with ASD may have difficulty anticipating future events, considering different options, and formulating plans accordingly. For example, a teenager with ASD may struggle to plan for upcoming assignments or activities, resulting in last-minute rushes or missed deadlines. Difficulties with planning can also impact social interactions, as individuals may struggle to anticipate the consequences of their actions or formulate appropriate responses in social situations.

Emotional regulation is another common EF challenge for individuals with ASD. Emotional regulation involves recognizing and managing one's own emotions in response to internal and external stimuli. Individuals with ASD may experience heightened emotional reactivity or difficulty in understanding and expressing their emotions effectively. For example, a child with ASD may become overwhelmed by sensory stimuli or frustrated by unexpected changes in routine, leading to emotional outbursts or meltdowns. Difficulties with emotional regulation can impact social interactions, as individuals may struggle to interpret others' emotions or regulate their own behavior in social situations.

Despite these challenges, individuals with ASD also possess unique strengths that can be leveraged to support the development of EF skills. One of these strengths is strong focus and attention to detail. Many individuals with ASD demonstrate an ability to focus intently on specific topics or tasks for extended periods, often exhibiting a high level of precision and accuracy in their work. For example, a teenager with ASD may excel in activities that require attention to detail, such as computer programming or artistic expression.

Additionally, individuals with ASD often demonstrate perseverance and determination in the face of challenges. They may exhibit a strong desire to master new skills or overcome obstacles, showing resilience and persistence in their efforts. For example, a child with ASD may work diligently to improve their social communication skills through role-playing exercises or social skills groups.

Furthermore, individuals with ASD may possess a unique ability to think in concrete and logical terms, which can be advantageous in problem-solving and decision-making tasks. They may excel in tasks that require systematic and analytical thinking, such as mathematics or computer programming. By leveraging this strength, individuals with ASD can develop strategies for approaching complex problems, breaking them down into manageable steps, and arriving at logical solutions.

CHAPTER 2

ASSESSMENT AND EVALUATION OF EXECUTIVE FUNCTIONING

ASSESSMENT TOOLS AND TECHNIQUES

Assessment of executive functioning (EF) skills in individuals with Autism Spectrum Disorder (ASD) is crucial for understanding their strengths and weaknesses, guiding intervention planning, and monitoring progress over time. Various assessment tools and techniques are employed to evaluate EF skills, ranging from standardized tests to informal observations and parent/teacher reports. Each method offers unique insights into the individual's EF profile, with its own set of strengths and limitations. Employing a multi-faceted approach that combines different assessment methods can provide a comprehensive understanding of the individual's EF functioning.

Standardized tests are one of the most common assessment tools used to evaluate EF skills in individuals with ASD. These tests often include tasks that measure various aspects of EF, such as working memory, inhibitory control, cognitive flexibility, and planning. Examples of standardized tests commonly used for assessing EF in individuals with ASD include the Behavior Rating Inventory of Executive Function

(BRIEF), the Delis-Kaplan Executive Function System (D-KEFS), and the Tower of London task.

The BRIEF is a questionnaire-based assessment completed by parents and teachers that evaluates EF skills in everyday life situations. It provides standardized scores across different domains of EF, allowing for comparison with typically developing peers. The D-KEFS is a comprehensive battery of tests that assess different aspects of EF through standardized tasks, such as sorting cards, generating novel ideas, and planning sequences of actions. The Tower of London task is a classic test of planning and problem-solving skills, where individuals are required to move colored beads on pegs to match a target arrangement, adhering to specific rules.

While standardized tests offer valuable insights into an individual's EF functioning, they also have limitations. Standardized tests may not fully capture the complexity and variability of EF deficits in individuals with ASD, as they often rely on structured tasks that may not reflect real-world challenges. Additionally, standardized tests may be influenced by factors such as language abilities, motivation, and test-taking skills, which can impact the validity of the results. Therefore, it is essential to interpret standardized test scores in conjunction with other assessment methods to gain a comprehensive understanding of the individual's EF profile.

Informal observations play a crucial role in assessing EF skills in individuals with ASD, as they allow for direct observation of the individual's behavior in naturalistic settings. Observations can be conducted in various contexts, such as the classroom, home, or community settings, and can provide valuable insights into the individual's EF functioning in everyday situations. Educators, parents, and other professionals can observe the individual's ability to plan and organize tasks, regulate emotions, and adapt to changes in the environment.

One advantage of informal observations is their ecological validity, as they capture the individual's behavior in real-world contexts. Observations also allow for the identification of specific situations or triggers that may impact the individual's EF functioning, informing targeted intervention planning. However, informal observations may be subject to bias and interpretation, as they rely on the observer's subjective impressions of the individual's behavior. Therefore, it is essential to supplement observations with other assessment methods to ensure a comprehensive evaluation of EF skills.

Parent and teacher reports are valuable sources of information for assessing EF skills in individuals with ASD. Parents and teachers have unique insights into the individual's behavior across different settings and can provide detailed information about the individual's EF functioning in everyday life. Questionnaires and rating scales, such as the BRIEF, are commonly used to gather information from parents and teachers about the individual's EF skills and behaviors.

Parent and teacher reports offer several advantages, including the ability to gather information from multiple sources and perspectives. Parents and teachers can provide valuable insights into the individual's behavior across different contexts, allowing for a more comprehensive understanding of their EF profile. However, parent and teacher reports may be influenced by factors such as the observer's own experiences, perceptions, and biases. Therefore, it is essential to consider multiple sources of information and triangulate data from different informants to ensure a comprehensive assessment of EF skills.

COLLABORATING WITH PROFESSIONALS FOR COMPREHENSIVE EVALUATION

Collaboration between parents, educators, and therapists is paramount in the assessment and evaluation of executive functioning (EF) skills in students with Autism Spectrum Disorder (ASD). Each professional brings unique expertise and perspectives to the evaluation process, contributing to a comprehensive understanding of the student's EF profile. Effective communication and collaboration among stakeholders are essential for ensuring that the evaluation process is thorough, holistic, and tailored to the individual student's needs.

Parents play a vital role in the assessment and evaluation of EF skills in students with ASD. They have intimate knowledge of their child's behavior, strengths, challenges, and preferences across different settings and contexts. Parents can provide valuable insights into their child's EF functioning in everyday life, including observations of behavior at home, interactions with family members, and participation in daily routines. Additionally, parents can offer information about their child's developmental history, medical background, and any previous assessments or interventions.

Educators also play a crucial role in the evaluation process, as they have firsthand experience working with the student in the school environment. Educators can observe the student's behavior in the classroom, interactions with peers, and performance on academic tasks. They can provide valuable insights into the student's EF skills related to organization, time management, task initiation, and social interaction. Educators can also administer standardized tests, conduct informal observations, and collaborate with other professionals to gather comprehensive data about the student's EF functioning.

Therapists, including speech-language pathologists, occupational therapists, and psychologists, bring specialized expertise to the evaluation of EF skills in students with ASD. They can administer standardized assessments, such as the Behavior Rating Inventory of Executive Function (BRIEF) or the Delis-Kaplan Executive Function System (D-KEFS), to measure specific aspects of EF. Therapists can also provide targeted interventions to address EF deficits, such as cognitive-behavioral therapy, social skills training, and sensory integration techniques.

Collaboration between parents, educators, and therapists is essential for ensuring that the evaluation process is comprehensive and integrated. By working together, professionals can share information, collaborate on assessment methods, and develop intervention plans that are tailored to the individual student's needs. Effective communication and collaboration among stakeholders can also help identify areas of strength and support the student's overall development and well-being.

To facilitate effective communication and collaboration between parents, educators, and therapists, it is essential to establish open lines of communication and maintain regular contact throughout the evaluation process. This can include scheduled meetings, phone calls, emails, and written progress reports. It is also important to establish a collaborative team approach, where all stakeholders are actively involved in decision-making and goal-setting.

When selecting assessment tools and strategies, it is important to consider the individual student's strengths, preferences, and learning style. Assessment methods should be chosen based on the student's unique needs and characteristics, with input from parents, educators, and therapists. For example, if a student has difficulty with verbal communication, alternative assessment methods, such as visual supports or interactive activities, may be more appropriate. Additionally, assessment tools should be culturally and linguistically appropriate, taking into account the student's background and experiences.

ETHICAL CONSIDERATION AND CHALLENGES

Assessing executive functioning (EF) skills in individuals with Autism Spectrum Disorder (ASD) involves navigating various ethical considerations to ensure the process is conducted responsibly and with sensitivity to the individual's needs and rights. Additionally, there are potential challenges and limitations associated with different assessment methods that must be addressed, along with guidance on interpreting assessment results and translating them into actionable strategies for intervention.

Ethical considerations in the assessment of EF skills in individuals with ASD encompass several key principles, including autonomy, beneficence, non-maleficence, justice, and respect for individuals' rights and dignity. It is essential to uphold these principles throughout the assessment process to ensure that individuals with ASD are treated with respect, fairness, and compassion.

One ethical consideration is obtaining informed consent from the individual or their legal guardian before conducting the assessment. Informed consent involves providing individuals or their guardians with clear and understandable information about the purpose, procedures, risks, and benefits of the assessment. This allows individuals and their guardians to make informed decisions about whether to participate in the assessment and to understand their rights and responsibilities.

Another ethical consideration is ensuring confidentiality and privacy throughout the assessment process. This includes safeguarding the confidentiality of assessment data and ensuring that sensitive information is only shared with authorized individuals involved in the individual's care. Professionals conducting the assessment should adhere to ethical guidelines and legal regulations regarding the storage, use, and dissemination of assessment data to protect the individual's privacy rights.

Additionally, it is essential to conduct the assessment in a culturally sensitive and linguistically appropriate manner. This involves considering the individual's cultural background, language preferences, and communication style when selecting assessment tools and interpreting results. Professionals should be mindful of cultural differences in attitudes toward disability, help-seeking behavior, and concepts of intelligence and academic achievement.

Furthermore, professionals conducting the assessment should strive to minimize any potential harm or distress to the individual with ASD. This includes using assessment methods and procedures that are developmentally appropriate, non-invasive, and respectful of the individual's sensory sensitivities and communication challenges. Professionals should also be sensitive to the emotional reactions that may arise during the assessment process and provide appropriate support and accommodations as needed.

Despite efforts to conduct assessments ethically and sensitively, there are potential challenges and limitations associated with different assessment methods that must be addressed. Standardized tests, for example, may not fully capture the complexity and variability of EF deficits in individuals with ASD. These tests often rely on structured tasks and may not accurately reflect the individual's EF skills in real-world settings.

Informal observations, while valuable for capturing the individual's behavior in naturalistic settings, may be subject to bias and interpretation. Observers may inadvertently impose their own assumptions or expectations onto the individual's behavior, leading to inaccuracies in assessment data. Additionally, informal observations may not provide standardized measures of EF skills, making it challenging to compare results across different individuals or settings.

Parent and teacher reports, while informative for gathering insights into the individual's behavior across different contexts, may also be influenced by subjective impressions and biases. Parents and teachers may have different perspectives on the individual's behavior, leading to discrepancies in reported observations.

Additionally, parent and teacher reports may be limited by factors such as recall bias, social desirability bias, and the quality of the parent-teacher relationship.

To mitigate these challenges and limitations, it is essential to adopt a multi-faceted approach to assessment that combines different methods and perspectives. This includes using a combination of standardized tests, informal observations, and parent/teacher reports to gather comprehensive data about the individual's EF skills. By triangulating data from multiple sources, professionals can obtain a more accurate and nuanced understanding of the individual's EF profile.

Interpreting assessment results and translating them into actionable strategies for intervention requires careful consideration of the individual's strengths, preferences, and learning style. It is essential to interpret assessment results within the context of the individual's developmental level, cultural background, and environmental factors. Professionals should consider the individual's unique needs and challenges when selecting intervention strategies and adapting them to fit the individual's strengths and preferences.

Additionally, collaboration with parents, educators, therapists, and other professionals is essential for developing effective intervention plans that address the individual's EF deficits comprehensively. By working together as a team, professionals can share expertise, resources, and support to implement interventions that promote the individual's overall well-being and success.

CHAPTER 3

STRATEGIES FOR BUILDING EXECUTIVE FUNCTIONING SKILLS

CREATING A SUPPORTIVE ENVIRONMENT

Creating a supportive learning and living environment is crucial for promoting the development of executive functioning (EF) skills in students with Autism Spectrum Disorder (ASD). These skills play a fundamental role in the student's ability to navigate academic tasks, social interactions, and daily routines effectively. By adapting the environment to address sensory sensitivities, create predictability, and reduce distractions, educators, caregivers, and other support professionals can create an environment that fosters the growth and success of students with ASD.

The importance of creating a supportive environment for students with ASD cannot be overstated. Individuals with ASD often experience sensory sensitivities, difficulty with transitions, and challenges with maintaining focus and attention. A supportive environment provides the necessary structure, support, and accommodations to help students with ASD thrive academically, socially, and emotionally.

One key aspect of creating a supportive environment for students with ASD is addressing sensory sensitivities. Many individuals with ASD are hypersensitive or hyposensitive to sensory stimuli, such as noise, light, textures, and smells. These sensory sensitivities can be overwhelming and distracting, making it difficult for students to focus, participate, and regulate their emotions.

To address sensory sensitivities, educators and caregivers can make modifications to the physical environment, such as reducing noise levels, adjusting lighting, and providing sensory-friendly materials and tools. For example, using noise-canceling headphones or providing fidget tools can help students with ASD regulate sensory input and maintain focus during classroom activities. Creating quiet zones or designated sensory break areas can also provide students with a safe space to retreat and recharge when feeling overwhelmed.

In addition to addressing sensory sensitivities, creating predictability and routine is essential for students with ASD. Many individuals with ASD thrive on structure and predictability, as it helps reduce anxiety and uncertainty. Establishing consistent routines, visual schedules, and clear expectations can provide students with ASD a sense of stability and control in their environment.

Visual supports, such as visual schedules, visual timers, and visual cues, can help students with ASD understand expectations and transitions more effectively. These supports provide a concrete and visual representation of the day's activities, helping students anticipate what will happen next and prepare for transitions accordingly. Consistency in routines and expectations also helps students with ASD feel more confident and secure in their environment, leading to improved engagement and participation.

Reducing distractions in the environment is another essential aspect of creating a supportive learning and living environment for students with ASD. Individuals with ASD may have difficulty filtering out irrelevant sensory information or maintaining attention in busy or chaotic environments. Minimizing visual and auditory distractions, such as clutter, excessive decorations, or loud noises, can help students with ASD stay focused and engaged in learning activities.

Educators can create a structured and organized classroom layout that minimizes visual clutter and provides clear pathways for movement. Using visual boundaries, such as rugs or tape on the floor, can help delineate different areas of the classroom and provide students with visual cues for spatial organization. Additionally, establishing consistent routines for transitions and activities can help reduce anxiety and improve predictability, leading to fewer disruptions and distractions in the learning environment.

Incorporating sensory-friendly elements into the environment, such as flexible seating options, calming sensory materials, and natural lighting, can also help create a supportive environment for students with ASD. Flexible seating allows students to choose seating options that best meet their sensory needs and preferences, promoting comfort and engagement during learning activities. Calming sensory materials, such as stress balls, weighted blankets, or sensory bins, provide students with opportunities for self-regulation and sensory exploration in a controlled and safe environment.

Natural lighting has been shown to positively impact mood, behavior, and attention in individuals with ASD. Maximizing natural light in the classroom and incorporating access to outdoor spaces can help create a calming and stimulating environment for students with

ASD. Providing opportunities for movement breaks, sensory breaks, and outdoor play can also help students regulate their energy levels and improve focus and attention during learning activities.

ESTABLISHING ROUTINES AND STRUCTURES

Establishing routines and structures is paramount for students with Autism Spectrum Disorder (ASD) as it plays a pivotal role in enhancing their planning, organization, and time management skills. Consistent routines provide predictability, reduce anxiety, and foster independence, ultimately facilitating the development of essential executive functioning (EF) skills.

The benefits of establishing routines and structures for students with ASD are multifaceted and extend to various aspects of their lives. One of the primary benefits is improved planning and organization skills. Routines provide a framework for students to anticipate and plan for upcoming activities, tasks, and transitions. By following a predictable schedule, students learn to allocate time effectively, prioritize tasks, and organize materials, thereby enhancing their ability to plan and manage their responsibilities independently.

Moreover, consistent routines contribute to the development of time management skills in students with ASD. By adhering to a structured schedule, students learn to gauge the passage of time, estimate how long tasks will take, and allocate time accordingly. This promotes a sense of time awareness and helps students develop the ability to pace themselves and complete tasks within designated time frames.

Additionally, routines and structures provide a sense of predictability and security for students with ASD, which can significantly reduce anxiety and stress. Many individuals with ASD thrive on predictability and struggle with uncertainty or unexpected changes. Consistent routines help create a sense of order and stability in the student's environment, allowing them to feel more comfortable and confident in navigating daily activities and transitions.

Practical Tips for Creating Visual Schedules:

Visual schedules are an effective tool for establishing routines and structures for students with ASD. They provide a visual representation of the day's activities, helping students understand what to expect and prepare for upcoming tasks and transitions. Here are some practical tips for creating visual schedules:

1. Use visual symbols or pictures to represent each activity or task: Choose simple, clear images that accurately depict each activity or task in the student's schedule. Use symbols or pictures that are meaningful and relevant to the student's interests and preferences.

2. Break down the schedule into manageable chunks: Divide the day into distinct time periods or blocks of time, and assign specific activities or tasks to each period. Breaking down the schedule into smaller chunks makes it easier for students to understand and follow.

3. Incorporate transition cues: Include visual cues or prompts to signal transitions between activities or tasks. This could include using arrows, lines, or color-coding to indicate the sequence of activities and transitions throughout the day.

4. Make the schedule accessible and portable: Ensure that the visual schedule is easily accessible to the student throughout the day. Consider using a portable visual schedule that can be carried or attached to the student's desk, backpack, or wheelchair for easy reference.

5. Review and update the schedule regularly: Review the visual schedule with the student at the beginning of each day to review the day's activities and expectations. Update the schedule as needed to reflect any changes or unexpected events that may arise.

Practical Tips for Breaking Down Tasks:

Breaking down tasks into smaller steps is another effective strategy for supporting students with ASD in following routines and completing tasks independently. Here are some practical tips for breaking down tasks:

1. Identify the steps involved in the task: Break down the task into its component steps or actions, starting with the first step and progressing sequentially to the final step.

2. Use visual or written prompts to guide the student through each step: Provide visual or written cues to remind the student of what needs to be done at each step of the task. This could include written instructions, pictures, or diagrams that illustrate each step of the task.

3. Provide modeling and demonstration: Demonstrate each step of the task yourself, and encourage the student to observe and imitate your actions. Use verbal prompts and gestures to reinforce key concepts and actions.

4. Offer support and encouragement: Provide positive reinforcement and encouragement as the student completes each step of the task. Offer praise, rewards, or incentives to motivate the student and reinforce their efforts.

5. Break tasks into manageable chunks: Break larger tasks into smaller, more manageable chunks to prevent overwhelm and promote success. Focus on one step at a time, and gradually increase the complexity or difficulty of the task as the student gains confidence and skill.

Practical Tips for Using Timers and Reminders:

Timers and reminders are valuable tools for helping students with ASD manage their time and stay on track with their routines and tasks. Here are some practical tips for using timers and reminders effectively:

1. Set clear expectations: Clearly communicate the purpose and expectations for using timers and reminders with the student. Explain how timers and reminders will be used to help them manage their time and stay organized.

2. Use visual or auditory timers: Choose timers that are easy for the student to understand and use. Visual timers, such as hourglasses or digital countdown timers, provide

a visual representation of the passage of time. Auditory timers, such as alarms or beepers, provide auditory cues to signal the end of a designated time period.

3. Set realistic time limits: Set appropriate time limits for tasks and activities based on the student's abilities and preferences. Break tasks into smaller time increments if needed, and gradually increase the duration as the student becomes more proficient.

4. Provide reminders and prompts: Use reminders and prompts to help the student stay focused and on task. This could include verbal reminders, written notes, or visual cues to prompt the student to start or finish a task.

5. Encourage self-monitoring: Teach the student to monitor their own time and use timers and reminders independently. Encourage the student to set their own timers and reminders for tasks and activities, and provide guidance and support as needed.

VISUAL SUPPORTS AND SCHEDULES

Visual supports and schedules play a pivotal role in supporting students with Autism Spectrum Disorder (ASD) by enhancing their understanding of expectations, managing transitions, and staying on task. These supports provide a visual framework that helps students with ASD comprehend information, anticipate upcoming events, and navigate daily routines more effectively. By utilizing various types of visual supports, such as pictures, charts, and checklists, educators and caregivers can create clear, concise, and individualized tools that cater to the unique needs of each student. Collaborating with students to ensure they understand and feel comfortable using visual supports is essential for maximizing their effectiveness and promoting independence.

Visual supports are highly effective for students with ASD as they capitalize on the visual learning strengths often associated with the condition. Visual information is processed more efficiently by the brain, making it easier for students with ASD to comprehend and retain information presented in visual formats. Additionally, visual supports provide concrete, tangible representations of abstract concepts, helping students with ASD grasp complex ideas and tasks more readily.

One of the primary benefits of visual supports is their ability to clarify expectations and facilitate understanding. For students with ASD who may struggle with verbal communication or abstract concepts, visual supports offer a clear and tangible way to convey information. Visual supports can be used to outline expectations for classroom behavior, academic tasks, social interactions, and daily routines.

Furthermore, visual supports are invaluable for managing transitions, which can be particularly challenging for students with ASD. Transitions between activities, changes in routines, and shifts in environments can be anxiety-provoking for students with ASD, leading to difficulties in maintaining focus and regulating emotions. Visual supports, such as visual schedules and transition cues, provide students with a predictable roadmap of what to expect, helping to ease anxiety and facilitate smoother transitions.

Visual schedules are one of the most commonly used types of visual supports for students with ASD. A visual schedule breaks down the day into manageable chunks, outlining the sequence of activities and transitions throughout the day. Visual schedules can be created using pictures, symbols, words, or a combination of these elements, depending on the student's preferences and needs. Each activity or task is represented visually, allowing students to see what will happen next and prepare accordingly.

In addition to visual schedules, other types of visual supports, such as picture charts and checklists, can also be beneficial for students with ASD. Picture charts provide visual step-by-step instructions for completing tasks or following routines. For example, a picture chart for getting ready in the morning may include images of brushing teeth, getting dressed, and eating breakfast in sequential order. Checklists offer a visual reminder of tasks that need to be completed, allowing students to track their progress and stay organized.

When creating and implementing visual supports for students with ASD, it is essential to ensure that they are clear, concise, and individualized to meet the specific needs of each student. Visual supports should be tailored to the student's developmental level, communication abilities, and sensory preferences. Consideration should also be given to the student's interests, strengths, and areas of challenge when selecting visual elements and formats.

Collaborating with students is crucial for ensuring that visual supports are meaningful and effective. Involve students in the process of creating and customizing visual supports to reflect their preferences and interests. Allow students to provide input on the types of visuals they find most helpful and engaging. By actively involving students in the selection and design of visual supports, educators empower them to take ownership of their learning and develop self-regulation skills.

In addition to collaborating with students, it is essential to provide explicit instruction and support for using visual supports effectively. Teach students how to use visual supports to anticipate upcoming events, follow routines, and track their progress. Model how to use visual supports and provide opportunities for guided practice and reinforcement. Encourage students to ask questions, seek clarification, and advocate for their needs when using visual supports.

Consistency is key when implementing visual supports for students with ASD. Visual supports should be used consistently across different settings and routines to reinforce learning and promote generalization of skills. Ensure that visual supports are easily accessible and prominently displayed in the classroom, home, or community environment. Review and update visual supports regularly to reflect changes in routines or activities.

TEACHING SELF-MONITORING AND SELF-REGULATION TECHNIQUES

Self-monitoring and self-regulation skills are essential for students with Autism Spectrum Disorder (ASD) to manage their emotions, control impulsive behaviors, and maintain focus. These skills enable students to become more independent, adaptable, and successful in various academic, social, and daily living situations. By teaching practical strategies and techniques for self-monitoring and self-regulation, educators and caregivers can empower students with ASD to better understand and manage their own thoughts, feelings, and behaviors.

The importance of self-monitoring and self-regulation skills for students with ASD cannot be overstated. Many individuals with ASD struggle with regulating their emotions, controlling impulsive behaviors, and maintaining focus due to challenges with social communication, sensory processing, and executive functioning. These difficulties can significantly impact their ability to function effectively in school, home, and community settings.

Self-monitoring involves the ability to observe and evaluate one's own thoughts, feelings, and behaviors in real-time. It requires self-awareness, reflection, and the ability to recognize when adjustments are needed. Self-regulation, on the other hand, involves the ability to control one's emotions, impulses, and responses in order to achieve goals and meet expectations. Self-regulation requires self-control, problem-solving skills, and the ability to cope with stress and frustration effectively.

Teaching self-monitoring and self-regulation skills to students with ASD is essential for promoting their overall well-being and success. By developing these skills, students can learn to manage their emotions, cope with challenges, and navigate social interactions more effectively. Self-monitoring and self-regulation skills also contribute to greater independence, autonomy, and self-advocacy, which are critical for success in school and beyond.

Practical strategies and techniques can be taught to help students with ASD develop self-monitoring and self-regulation skills. These strategies provide students with tools and techniques to recognize and manage their own thoughts, feelings, and behaviors in various situations. Examples of self-monitoring strategies include self-talk, self-assessment tools, and calming techniques.

Self-talk involves using internal dialogue to guide and regulate one's thoughts and behaviors. Encouraging students to use positive self-talk can help them challenge negative thoughts, manage stress, and stay focused on their goals. For example, students can use phrases like "I can do this," "Take a deep breath," or "Stay calm" to reassure themselves and stay on track during challenging situations.

Self-assessment tools are another valuable strategy for promoting self-monitoring and self-regulation skills. These tools allow students to reflect on their own thoughts, feelings, and behaviors and identify areas for improvement. For example, students can use checklists, rating scales, or journals to track their progress, set goals, and monitor their own behavior over time.

Calming techniques are essential for helping students with ASD regulate their emotions and manage stress and anxiety effectively. Teaching students relaxation techniques, such as deep breathing, progressive muscle relaxation, or mindfulness exercises, can help them calm their minds and bodies when feeling overwhelmed or agitated. Encouraging students to practice these techniques regularly can help build resilience and coping skills over time.

In addition to teaching specific self-monitoring and self-regulation strategies, it is important to incorporate social-emotional learning (SEL) into the curriculum to foster the development of these skills. SEL promotes self-awareness, self-management, social awareness, relationship skills, and responsible decision-making, all of which are essential components of self-monitoring and self-regulation.

Integrating SEL into the curriculum provides students with opportunities to learn and practice social and emotional skills in a supportive and structured environment. Activities such as role-playing, group discussions, and cooperative learning exercises can help students develop empathy, communication skills, and conflict resolution strategies. SEL also helps create a positive classroom climate where students feel valued, respected, and supported in their social and emotional development.

CHAPTER 4

ENHANCING PLANNING AND ORGANIZATION SKILLS

BREAKING TASKS INTO MANAGEABLE STEPS

Breaking tasks into manageable steps is crucial for students with Autism Spectrum Disorder (ASD) to improve their planning and organization skills. Many individuals with ASD face cognitive challenges related to task initiation, planning, and problem-solving, making it difficult for them to tackle large tasks independently. By breaking tasks into smaller, more manageable steps, educators and caregivers can help students with ASD overcome these challenges and build the skills they need to succeed academically, socially, and in daily living activities.

Individuals with ASD often struggle with executive functioning skills, which encompass a range of cognitive processes involved in planning, organizing, and executing tasks. Task initiation, planning, and problem-solving are particularly challenging for many individuals with ASD due to difficulties with cognitive flexibility, working memory, and abstract thinking. These cognitive challenges can make it overwhelming for students with ASD to approach large tasks or complex activities, leading to procrastination, avoidance, or frustration.

Breaking tasks into smaller, more manageable steps is essential for helping students with ASD overcome these cognitive challenges and build their planning and organization skills. By breaking tasks down into discrete steps, educators and caregivers provide students with a clear and structured framework for approaching tasks systematically. This helps reduce feelings of overwhelm and uncertainty, making tasks more approachable and achievable for students with ASD.

Also, breaking tasks down into smaller steps helps students with ASD develop a sense of mastery and accomplishment as they progress through each step. This incremental approach allows students to focus on one manageable task at a time, building confidence and momentum as they work towards completing the larger task. Celebrating small victories along the way reinforces positive self-esteem and motivates students to continue their efforts.

Practical strategies for breaking tasks down include using graphic organizers, flowcharts, or visual aids to visually represent the steps involved in the task. Graphic organizers provide a visual framework for organizing information and breaking down complex tasks into smaller components. For example, a flowchart can illustrate the sequence of steps involved in completing a multi-step task, such as solving a math problem or following a recipe. Visual aids, such as pictures, diagrams, or written instructions, can also help students understand and remember each step of the task more easily.

Teaching students to prioritize tasks and estimate the time needed to complete them is essential for effective task management. Students with ASD may struggle with prioritizing tasks and allocating their time and resources effectively. By teaching students to identify and prioritize tasks based on importance, urgency, and deadlines, educators and caregivers help students develop decision-making skills and allocate their time more efficiently.

Likewise, teaching students to estimate the time needed to complete each step of a task helps them develop realistic expectations and manage their time effectively. Encouraging students to break tasks down into smaller time increments and allocate specific amounts of time to each step helps prevent procrastination and ensures that students make steady progress towards completing the task.

In addition to breaking tasks down into manageable steps, it is essential to provide scaffolding and support to help students with ASD develop their planning and organization skills. This may involve providing verbal prompts, written instructions, or modeling strategies for breaking tasks down and managing their time effectively. Gradually fading support as students become more proficient helps build independence and self-regulation skills over time.

Moreover, providing opportunities for practice and reinforcement is essential for helping students with ASD generalize their skills to new tasks and contexts. Integrating task management skills into daily routines and academic activities helps students apply their skills in real-world situations and develop greater independence and autonomy.

USING TASK LISTS AND CHECKLISTS

Using task lists and checklists is highly effective for helping students with Autism Spectrum Disorder (ASD) plan their work, organize their belongings, and track their progress. These tools provide a structured framework for managing tasks and responsibilities, helping students with ASD overcome challenges related to memory recall, executive functioning, and anxiety.

Task lists and checklists are highly effective tools for students with ASD as they provide a visual representation of tasks and responsibilities, making them easier to understand and manage. Many individuals with ASD struggle with executive functioning skills, such as planning, organization, and time management, which can make it challenging for them to remember and prioritize tasks independently. Task lists and checklists offer a structured approach to managing tasks, helping students break down complex activities into smaller, more manageable steps.

One of the key benefits of using task lists and checklists is their ability to improve memory recall and reduce anxiety related to managing multiple tasks. Students with ASD may have difficulty remembering tasks, deadlines, and instructions due to challenges with working memory and cognitive flexibility. Task lists and checklists serve as external memory aids, providing students with a concrete reminder of what needs to be done and when. By offloading the burden of remembering tasks, students can focus their cognitive resources on completing tasks more effectively, reducing feelings of overwhelm and anxiety.

Task lists and checklists help students with ASD organize their belongings and materials, promoting greater independence and efficiency. Many students with ASD struggle with organization skills, leading to cluttered desks, lost assignments, and difficulty finding necessary materials. Task lists and checklists provide a systematic approach to organizing materials, ensuring that students have everything they need to complete tasks and assignments successfully.

There are various types of task lists and checklists that can be adapted to different needs and preferences. Paper-based lists, such as written checklists or to-do lists, are a simple and accessible option for students who prefer tangible materials. Students can write down tasks, deadlines, and instructions on a piece of paper or in a notebook, checking off items as they are completed. Paper-based lists can be personalized to meet the individual needs of each student, allowing for flexibility and customization.

Digital task lists and checklists offer another option for students who prefer technology-based solutions. Digital apps and platforms, such as productivity apps, task management software, or calendar apps, provide students with a convenient way to organize tasks and track their progress. Digital tools offer features such as reminders, notifications, and syncing across devices, making it easier for students to stay organized and on track with their responsibilities.

Visual task lists and checklists are particularly beneficial for students with ASD who are visual learners or prefer visual supports. Visual lists use pictures, symbols, or icons to represent tasks and instructions, making them more accessible and understandable for students with ASD. Visual lists can be created using graphic organizers, visual schedules, or picture charts, allowing students to see what needs to be done at a glance and track their progress visually.

Teaching students how to create and use task lists and checklists effectively is essential for maximizing their benefits. Educators and caregivers can provide explicit instruction and modeling on how to create and organize task lists, prioritize tasks, and use checklists to track progress. Encouraging students to break tasks down into smaller steps and set realistic goals helps students develop effective planning and organization skills. Additionally, providing opportunities for practice and reinforcement helps students internalize these strategies and apply them in various contexts.

Moreover, it is important to teach students how to monitor and adjust their task lists and checklists as needed. Encouraging students to review their lists regularly, update them with new tasks or changes, and reflect on their progress helps build metacognitive awareness and self-regulation skills. Students can learn to identify barriers or challenges they may encounter, problem-solve solutions, and adjust their plans accordingly.

ORGANIZATIONAL SYSTEMS AND TOOLS

Organizational systems and tools are invaluable resources for students with Autism Spectrum Disorder (ASD) as they provide structure, support, and clarity in managing tasks, time, and information. From traditional planners and calendars to modern assistive technology tools, there is a wide range of options available to help students with ASD effectively organize their lives and succeed academically, socially, and in daily living activities.

Planners and organizers are classic organizational tools that can be highly beneficial for students with ASD. Planners allow students to record their assignments, deadlines, appointments, and other important information in one centralized location, helping them stay organized and on track with their responsibilities. Organizers, such as binders or folders, provide a physical system for storing and categorizing materials, notes, and handouts, reducing clutter and facilitating easy access to information.

Calendars are another essential organizational tool for students with ASD as they provide a visual representation of time and help students schedule their activities effectively. Calendars allow students to record upcoming events, deadlines, and commitments, providing a structured framework for planning and prioritizing tasks. Digital calendars offer additional features such as reminders, notifications, and syncing across devices, making it easier for students to manage their schedules and stay organized.

Filing systems are valuable organizational tools for students with ASD as they provide a systematic approach to storing and retrieving information. Filing systems allow students to categorize and label documents, assignments, and resources, making it easier to locate specific materials when needed. Color-coding files or using visual labels can help students with ASD navigate the filing system more effectively and reduce confusion.

Assistive technology tools offer additional support for students with ASD in organizing their lives and managing their responsibilities. Technology-based tools, such as task management apps, note-taking software, or speech-to-text programs, provide students with flexible and customizable options for organizing tasks, information, and resources. These tools offer features such as reminders, alarms, and notifications, helping students stay on track and manage their time effectively.

The benefits of organizational systems and tools for students with ASD are numerous and significant. These tools provide structure, predictability, and clarity, which are essential for individuals with ASD who may struggle with executive functioning skills, such as planning, organization, and time management. By utilizing organizational systems and tools, students with ASD can develop greater independence, accountability, and self-regulation, ultimately leading to improved academic performance, social interactions, and daily living skills.

When choosing and implementing organizational systems for students with ASD, it is important to consider their individual needs, preferences, and learning styles. Some students may prefer paper-based systems, while others may thrive with digital tools. It is essential to involve students in the decision-making process and tailor organizational systems to meet their unique needs and preferences.

For younger students with ASD, simple and visually appealing organizational systems may be most effective. Using color-coded folders, picture schedules, or tactile markers can help younger students understand and navigate organizational systems more easily. Providing clear and explicit instructions on how to use organizational tools and incorporating visual supports can help younger students develop independence and confidence in managing their responsibilities.

For older students with ASD, more sophisticated organizational systems and tools may be appropriate.

Digital planners, task management apps, or cloud-based storage systems offer flexibility and customization options that may appeal to older students. Providing opportunities for students to explore different organizational tools and find what works best for them can help foster independence and self-advocacy.

Regardless of the age group or learning style, it is crucial to teach students how to use organizational systems effectively and consistently. Providing explicit instruction, modeling, and guided practice can help students develop the skills they need to navigate organizational tools independently. Encouraging students to establish routines, set goals, and review their organizational systems regularly helps reinforce their use and promote accountability.

Moreover, it is essential to provide ongoing support and encouragement as students learn to use organizational systems. Acknowledging their progress, celebrating their successes, and providing constructive feedback helps motivate students and build their confidence in managing their responsibilities. Creating a supportive and inclusive environment where students feel empowered to ask questions, seek assistance, and advocate for their needs fosters a positive attitude towards organizational systems and promotes continued growth and development.

CHAPTER 5

DEVELOPING TIME MANAGEMENT SKILLS

UNDERSTANDING THE CONCEPT OF TIME

Understanding the concept of time poses significant challenges for individuals with Autism Spectrum Disorder (ASD) due to difficulties with abstract thinking, executive functioning, and sensory processing. Time is a complex and abstract concept that encompasses various dimensions, including past, present, future, duration, and sequence. Individuals with ASD may struggle to grasp these concepts and apply them in daily life, leading to difficulties with planning, organization, time management, and understanding social cues.

Individuals with ASD often struggle with abstract thinking, which can make it challenging for them to understand concepts that are not tangible or concrete. Time is inherently abstract, as it cannot be seen, touched, or directly experienced. Understanding abstract concepts like past, present, and future requires the ability to mentally manipulate and sequence events in time, which can be difficult for individuals with ASD who may have difficulty with cognitive flexibility and working memory.

Individuals with ASD may have difficulties with executive functioning skills, such as planning, organization, and time management, which further compound their challenges with understanding the concept of time. Difficulties with executive functioning can make it challenging for individuals with ASD to anticipate future events, estimate time accurately, and plan and prioritize tasks effectively.

Sensory processing differences also play a role in the challenges individuals with ASD face in understanding the concept of time. Many individuals with ASD have sensory sensitivities or differences, which can affect their perception of time and their ability to focus and attend to temporal cues. Sensory overload or distraction may interfere with individuals' ability to perceive the passage of time or maintain attention on tasks for extended periods.

Given the complex and abstract nature of time, it is essential to break down the concept into concrete, visual, and relatable components to help individuals with ASD understand and apply it in daily life. One way to do this is by using visual aids, such as calendars, clocks, timers, and schedules, to provide concrete representations of time and temporal concepts.

Calendars are valuable tools for helping individuals with ASD understand the passage of time and anticipate future events. Visual calendars with clear labels, color-coding, and symbols can help individuals visualize upcoming events, deadlines, and routines. Daily, weekly, and monthly calendars can be used to provide different levels of detail and structure, depending on the individual's needs and preferences.

Clocks and timers are another essential tool for teaching the concept of time to individuals with ASD. Analog clocks with clear markings and hands can help individuals understand the passage of time in relation to the position of the hands. Digital clocks and timers provide visual feedback and auditory cues to help individuals track time and manage tasks more effectively. Using timers for activities and transitions helps individuals understand the duration of tasks and develop a sense of time management.

Visual schedules and routines are effective tools for helping individuals with ASD understand the sequence of events and anticipate what will happen next. Visual schedules use pictures, symbols, or written words to represent activities, tasks, and routines in sequential order. Breaking down daily routines into smaller steps and providing visual cues for each step helps individuals understand the sequence of events and navigate transitions more effectively.

Hands-on activities and real-life experiences are also valuable for teaching the concept of time to individuals with ASD. Engaging in activities such as cooking, gardening, or arts and crafts that involve planning, sequencing, and time management helps individuals develop a tangible understanding of time and its practical applications. Incorporating time-related vocabulary and concepts into everyday activities helps reinforce learning and promote generalization of skills.

It is important to tailor teaching strategies and materials to meet the individual needs and preferences of each student with ASD. Some students may benefit from highly structured and visually explicit materials, while others may prefer more flexible and interactive approaches. Providing opportunities for hands-on exploration, guided practice, and reinforcement helps individuals with ASD develop a deeper understanding of the concept of time and its relevance to their daily lives.

Moreover, it is essential to provide ongoing support and encouragement as individuals with ASD learn to understand and apply the concept of time. Acknowledging their efforts, celebrating their progress, and providing positive reinforcement help motivate individuals and build their confidence in managing time-related tasks and activities. Creating a supportive and inclusive environment where individuals feel valued, respected, and empowered to ask questions, seek assistance, and advocate for their needs fosters a positive attitude towards learning and promotes continued growth and development.

TEACHING TIME MANAGEMENT STRATEGIES

Teaching time management skills to students with Autism Spectrum Disorder (ASD) is essential for fostering independence, organization, and success in various aspects of life. Individuals with ASD often struggle with executive functioning skills, including planning, organization, and time management, making it challenging for them to effectively manage their time and complete tasks in a timely manner. However, by implementing various strategies tailored to their needs, educators and caregivers can empower students with

ASD to develop effective time management skills and thrive academically, socially, and in daily living activities.

One of the key strategies for teaching time management to students with ASD is breaking tasks down into smaller, more manageable chunks. Many individuals with ASD struggle with task initiation, planning, and organization, making it difficult for them to approach large tasks or complex activities independently. Breaking tasks into smaller steps provides students with a clear and structured framework for approaching tasks systematically, reducing feelings of overwhelm and uncertainty.

Educators and caregivers can help students break tasks down into smaller chunks by providing explicit instructions, modeling the process, and using visual aids such as checklists or graphic organizers. Breaking tasks down into smaller steps allows students to focus on one manageable task at a time, building confidence and momentum as they work towards completing the larger task. Celebrating small victories along the way reinforces positive self-esteem and motivates students to continue their efforts.

Another important strategy for teaching time management to students with ASD is estimating the time needed for completion. Many individuals with ASD struggle with estimating time accurately, leading to difficulties with planning, prioritizing, and allocating their time effectively. Teaching students how to estimate the time needed for different tasks helps them develop realistic expectations and manage their time more efficiently.

Educators and caregivers can help students estimate time by providing examples, practicing with timers, and reflecting on past experiences. Using timers for activities and transitions helps students understand the duration of tasks and develop a sense of time management. Encouraging students to break tasks down into smaller time increments and allocate specific amounts of time to each step helps prevent procrastination and ensures that students make steady progress towards completing the task.

Creating visual schedules and reminders is another effective strategy for teaching time management to students with ASD. Visual schedules use pictures, symbols, or written words to represent activities, tasks, and routines in sequential order, providing students with a visual roadmap for their day. Visual schedules help students understand the sequence of events, anticipate what will happen next, and manage their time more effectively.

Educators and caregivers can create visual schedules using whiteboards, calendars, or digital apps, depending on the individual's needs and preferences. Providing clear and consistent routines helps students develop a sense of predictability and stability, reducing anxiety and increasing their ability to manage their time independently. Using visual reminders, such as alarms or notifications, helps students stay on track and transition between activities more smoothly.

Using timers is another valuable strategy for teaching time management to students with ASD. Timers provide students with a concrete representation of time and help them understand the passage of time more effectively. Using timers for activities and transitions helps students pace themselves, stay focused, and manage their time more efficiently. Timers also provide a sense of structure and predictability, helping students develop a routine and stick to a schedule.

Educators and caregivers can use a variety of timers, such as analog clocks, digital timers, or timer apps, depending on the individual's needs and preferences. Setting clear expectations and providing feedback on time management skills helps students develop self-awareness and accountability. Using timers consistently and gradually increasing time expectations helps students build.

USING TIMERS AND ALARMS EFFECTIVELY

Using timers and alarms effectively can be incredibly beneficial for students with Autism Spectrum Disorder (ASD) in managing their time, staying on task, and improving overall productivity. By implementing timers and alarms strategically, educators and caregivers can provide structure, support, and motivation for students with ASD to manage their time effectively and achieve their goals.

Timers and alarms offer several benefits for students with ASD in managing their time and staying on task. Firstly, timers provide a tangible representation of time passing, helping students understand the passage of time more concretely. Many individuals with ASD struggle with abstract concepts like time, so having a visual or auditory cue can make it easier for them to comprehend and adhere to time limits. Additionally, timers can serve as a helpful tool for transitioning between activities, as students can visually or audibly see when one task ends and another begins.

Timers and alarms can help students with ASD improve their time management skills by providing structure and accountability. By setting specific time limits for tasks or activities, students are encouraged to work efficiently and stay focused within the allotted timeframe. This can help prevent procrastination and increase productivity, as students are motivated to complete tasks within the designated time period.

Timers and alarms can also be useful for students with ASD who may struggle with attention and focus. By setting timers or alarms at regular intervals, students can break tasks into smaller, more manageable chunks and take short breaks as needed. This can help prevent sensory overload or fatigue and maintain optimal levels of attention and engagement throughout the day.

There are various types of timers and alarms available, each with its own features and benefits. Analog timers, such as kitchen timers or hourglasses, provide a visual representation of time passing and can be helpful for students who prefer tactile or hands-on tools. Digital timers offer more precise control over time intervals and often include additional features such as countdown timers, alarms, and customizable settings.

Timer apps and software are another option for students with ASD, offering flexibility and convenience for setting timers on digital devices such as smartphones, tablets, or computers. Many timer apps allow users to customize settings, choose different sounds or visuals for alarms, and track time intervals for specific tasks or activities. Timer apps can be particularly useful for students who are more comfortable using technology or prefer digital tools.

When choosing the most appropriate timers and alarms for students with ASD, it is important that you consider their individual needs, preferences, and sensory sensitivities. Some students may prefer analog timers for their simplicity and tactile feedback, while others may prefer digital timers for their precision and customizable features. Similarly, some students may respond better to auditory alarms, while others may find visual cues more effective.

In addition to selecting the right type of timer or alarm, it is essential to provide guidance on setting and using them effectively. For students with ASD, it can be helpful to pair timers with visual cues or prompts to reinforce time management skills. This could involve using visual schedules, checklists, or written instructions to indicate when and how long to set the timer for specific tasks or activities.

Gradually increasing time intervals and allowing for breaks as needed can also help students with ASD build endurance and resilience over time. Start with shorter time intervals and gradually increase them as students become more comfortable with managing their time and staying on task. Encouraging students to take short breaks between tasks can help prevent burnout and maintain motivation and focus throughout the day.

You must provide positive reinforcement and praise for students' efforts and achievements in using timers and alarms effectively. Acknowledging their progress, celebrating their successes, and providing constructive feedback help motivate students and build their confidence in managing their time independently.

CHAPTER 6

IMPROVING FLEXIBILITY AND ADAPTABILITY

UNDERSTANDING RIGIDITY AND FLEXIBILITY IN AUTISM

Understanding rigidity and flexibility in Autism Spectrum Disorder (ASD) is very important for recognizing and addressing the unique challenges individuals with ASD face in navigating their environment and daily interactions. Rigidity refers to a cognitive and behavioral inflexibility characterized by adherence to routines, resistance to change, and difficulty adapting to unexpected situations. It is closely linked to the core characteristics of ASD, including challenges with social communication, sensory processing, and cognitive flexibility.

Individuals with ASD often exhibit rigidity in their behavior and thinking patterns, which can manifest in various ways across different contexts. Rigidity is rooted in the neurodevelopmental differences associated with ASD, including atypical brain connectivity, sensory processing difficulties, and challenges with executive functioning. These differences affect how individuals with ASD perceive and respond to their environment, leading to a preference for sameness, predictability, and routine.

One of the key characteristics of rigidity in ASD is a strong attachment to routines and rituals. Individuals with ASD may adhere rigidly to specific routines or rituals in their daily activities, such as following the same schedule, eating the same foods, or engaging in repetitive behaviors. Deviations from these routines can cause distress or anxiety, as individuals with ASD may struggle to cope with unexpected changes or disruptions to their familiar environment.

Moreover, individuals with ASD may have difficulty adapting to changes in their environment or routines. They may become overwhelmed or anxious when faced with new or unfamiliar situations, as they may struggle to anticipate and prepare for the changes. This difficulty adapting to changes can impact various aspects of daily life, including transitions between activities, changes in plans, or disruptions to familiar routines.

Sensory processing differences also contribute to rigidity in individuals with ASD. Many individuals with ASD have heightened sensory sensitivity or sensory-seeking behaviors, which can affect how they experience and respond to sensory stimuli in their environment. Sensory overload or discomfort may trigger rigidity in behavior, as individuals with ASD may seek to control their environment or avoid sensory triggers that cause distress.

Furthermore, individuals with ASD may have difficulty with abstract thinking and problem-solving, which can contribute to rigidity in their thinking patterns. They may struggle to understand abstract concepts, interpret ambiguous situations, or consider alternative perspectives, leading to rigid and black-and-white thinking. This cognitive inflexibility can make it challenging for individuals with ASD to adapt to new information or changes in their environment.

The need for predictability and control is another factor underlying rigidity in ASD. Individuals with ASD may have a strong need for predictability and control in their environment to feel safe and secure. They may rely on familiar routines and rituals as a way of coping with uncertainty and reducing anxiety. Any disruptions to their routine or changes in their environment can disrupt their sense of predictability and control, leading to rigidity in behavior.

Additionally, social communication difficulties can contribute to rigidity in individuals with ASD. Challenges with understanding social cues, interpreting others' intentions, and responding flexibly in social situations can lead to rigid and rule-bound behavior. Individuals with ASD may struggle to adapt their behavior to different social contexts or understand the perspectives of others, leading to social isolation or misunderstandings.

The challenges associated with rigidity in ASD can have significant implications for individuals' daily functioning, social interactions, and quality of life. Difficulty adapting to changes or unexpected situations can lead to stress, anxiety, and frustration for individuals with ASD and their families. It can also impact their ability to participate in everyday activities, access educational or employment opportunities, and engage in meaningful social relationships.

Educators, caregivers, and professionals working with individuals with ASD play a crucial role in supporting flexibility and adaptive behavior. By understanding the underlying reasons behind rigidity in ASD and implementing targeted interventions, they can help individuals with ASD develop coping strategies, build resilience, and navigate their environment more effectively.

One approach to promoting flexibility in individuals with ASD is through the use of visual supports and structured routines. Visual schedules, checklists, and social stories can help individuals anticipate changes, understand expectations, and prepare for transitions in their environment. Providing clear and consistent routines helps establish predictability and reduces anxiety, allowing individuals with ASD to feel more comfortable and confident in their surroundings.

Additionally, incorporating opportunities for choice and autonomy can help individuals with ASD develop a sense of control and agency over their environment. Offering choices within structured routines, such as selecting preferred activities or materials, empowers individuals with ASD to make decisions and take ownership of their actions. This promotes flexibility and adaptive behavior, as individuals learn to navigate their environment and make choices that meet their needs and preferences.

Teaching problem-solving and coping skills is another important aspect of promoting flexibility in individuals with ASD. By teaching individuals how to identify problems, generate solutions, and adapt their strategies based on changing circumstances, educators and caregivers can help individuals develop greater resilience and adaptability. Role-playing and social skills training can also provide opportunities for individuals to practice flexible thinking and problem-solving in social situations.

Likewise, providing support and encouragement for trying new things and taking risks is essential for promoting flexibility in individuals with ASD. Celebrating small successes, acknowledging efforts, and providing positive reinforcement for adaptive behavior help build confidence and motivation. Creating a supportive and accepting environment where individuals feel valued and respected encourages them to explore new experiences and develop their skills.

STRATEGIES FOR TEACHING FLEXIBILITY

Flexibility and adaptability are crucial skills for individuals with Autism Spectrum Disorder (ASD) to navigate the complexities of everyday life. Teaching flexibility involves helping students with ASD develop the ability to cope with changes, manage transitions, and respond appropriately to unexpected situations. Given the cognitive and sensory challenges often associated with ASD, it is essential to implement strategies that promote flexibility in a supportive and structured manner.

One effective strategy for teaching flexibility to students with ASD is to introduce changes gradually and predictably. Individuals with ASD often thrive on routine and predictability, so abrupt changes can be overwhelming and distressing. By gradually introducing changes and providing advanced notice, we can help students with ASD prepare for transitions and adapt more easily to new situations. For example, if a change in routine is anticipated, we can provide visual schedules or calendars to help students understand and prepare for the upcoming change. Additionally, using social stories or role-playing scenarios can help students practice coping strategies and problem-solving skills in response to changes.

Providing visual cues and social stories is another effective strategy for teaching flexibility to students with ASD. Visual supports, such as schedules, checklists, and visual timers, provide concrete and tangible reminders of upcoming transitions or changes in routine. These visual cues help students with ASD understand what to expect and prepare for the transition in advance. Social stories, which use simple language and visual illustrations to explain social situations or expectations, can also help students with ASD understand why changes occur and how to respond appropriately. For example, a social story may explain that unexpected changes can happen, but it's essential to stay calm and flexible in these situations.

Incorporating activities that promote problem-solving and perspective-taking is essential for teaching flexibility to students with ASD. Problem-solving activities encourage students to identify challenges, brainstorm solutions, and evaluate the consequences of different actions. This helps students develop critical thinking skills and learn to adapt their strategies based on changing circumstances. Perspective-taking activities help students understand different points of view and consider alternative perspectives, which is crucial for developing empathy and flexibility in social interactions. For example, we can facilitate role-playing scenarios where students take on different roles and perspectives to practice flexible thinking and problem-solving skills.

Specific examples of activities and interventions that can be used to teach flexibility to students with ASD include:

Role-playing scenarios: We can create role-playing scenarios that simulate real-life situations where flexibility is required, such as changes in routine, unexpected events, or social conflicts. Students can take on different roles and practice responding flexibly to the situation, considering alternative perspectives, and finding solutions to the problem.

Social skills groups: Social skills groups provide a structured and supportive environment for students with ASD to practice social interactions and communication skills. Within these groups, we can incorporate activities that focus on flexibility, such as cooperative games, group projects, and problem-solving exercises. These activities help students learn to collaborate with others, adapt to different social contexts, and navigate conflicts effectively.

Introducing unexpected elements into familiar routines: We can intentionally introduce unexpected elements or changes into familiar routines to help students with ASD learn to cope with uncertainty and adaptability. For example, we can vary the order of activities within a daily schedule, introduce new materials or tasks during a familiar activity, or change the location or format of a lesson. These unexpected changes provide opportunities for students to practice flexibility and problem-solving skills in a controlled and supportive environment.

Providing positive reinforcement and praise: Reinforcing flexible behavior with positive reinforcement and praise helps motivate students and reinforce the importance of flexibility in everyday life. We can praise students for their efforts to adapt to changes, cope with unexpected situations, and demonstrate flexible thinking. Celebrating small successes and progress towards flexibility goals encourages continued growth and development in this area.

CHAPTER 7

WORKING WITH PARENTS AND CAREGIVERS

BUILDING PARTNERSHIPS WITH FAMILIES

Building strong partnerships with families is essential for creating a supportive and collaborative environment for individuals with ASD. Parents and caregivers are valuable members of the intervention team and have unique insights into their child's strengths, challenges, and preferences. By involving parents and caregivers in the intervention process, educators and professionals can gain a deeper understanding of the individual's needs and develop more effective intervention plans.

Effective communication is the foundation of building partnerships with families. It is essential to establish open, honest, and respectful communication channels with parents and caregivers from the beginning. This includes actively listening to their concerns, acknowledging their expertise and insights, and involving them in decision-making processes related to their child's education and support needs.

Additionally, educators and professionals should strive to create a welcoming and inclusive environment that fosters collaboration and trust. This may involve inviting parents and caregivers to participate in meetings, workshops, and school events, and providing opportunities for them to connect with other families and professionals in the community. Building a sense of community and belonging can help parents and caregivers feel supported and empowered to advocate for their child's needs.

PROVIDING RESOURCES AND SUPPORT FOR PARENTS

Parents and caregivers of individuals with ASD often face unique challenges and may require additional support and resources to navigate the complexities of raising a child with ASD. Educators and professionals can play a vital role in providing parents with access to information, resources, and support services to help them better understand their child's diagnosis, access interventions and therapies, and navigate the education system.

One way to support parents is by providing access to accurate and reliable information about ASD. This may include sharing educational materials, online resources, and workshops or training sessions on topics related to ASD, such as understanding the diagnosis, accessing services and supports, and advocating for their child's needs.

In addition to informational resources, parents and caregivers may benefit from emotional support and peer networks. Establishing support groups or parent networks where parents can connect with others who share similar experiences can provide valuable opportunities for mutual support, encouragement, and sharing of resources and strategies.

COLLABORATING ON STRATEGIES FOR HOME AND SCHOOL

Collaboration between home and school is essential for ensuring consistency and continuity of support for individuals with ASD. Educators and professionals should work closely with parents and caregivers to develop and implement strategies that support the individual's learning, development, and overall well-being across home and school settings.

One way to promote collaboration between home and school is by developing and sharing individualized intervention plans or behavior support plans. These plans outline specific goals, strategies, and interventions tailored to the individual's unique needs and preferences, and are developed collaboratively with input from both home and school stakeholders.

Regular communication between home and school is also critical for maintaining alignment and addressing any concerns or challenges that may arise. This may include regular progress updates, check-ins, and opportunities for parents and caregivers to provide feedback on their child's progress and experiences in school.

Furthermore, educators and professionals should collaborate with parents and caregivers to identify and implement strategies that support the individual's learning and development at home. This may involve providing parents with resources, materials, and strategies to reinforce learning goals and skills taught in school, as well as offering guidance on how to create a supportive and structured environment at home.

CONCLUSION

In closing, this book has aimed to provide comprehensive insights, strategies, and guidance for supporting individuals with Autism Spectrum Disorder (ASD) across various contexts. From understanding the unique challenges faced by individuals with ASD to implementing effective intervention strategies in educational and home settings, each chapter has been crafted with the utmost care and attention to detail.

As readers, your engagement with the material presented in this book signifies a commitment to enhancing the lives of individuals with ASD and promoting their well-being and success. Your dedication to learning and implementing evidence-based practices underscores the importance of collaborative efforts in supporting individuals with ASD to reach their fullest potential.

As you reflect on the knowledge gained from this book and begin to apply it in your professional or personal life, I encourage you to consider sharing your thoughts and experiences by leaving a positive review and a thoughtful rating on Amazon. Your feedback not only serves as valuable encouragement for the authors and contributors but also helps other readers make informed decisions about the book's relevance and impact.

By leaving a positive review and rating, you contribute to the broader community of professionals, caregivers, and individuals affected by ASD, fostering a culture of support, understanding, and empowerment. Together, we can continue to advocate for the needs of individuals with ASD and promote inclusivity, acceptance, and opportunity for all.

Thank you for your dedication, passion, and commitment to making a difference in the lives of individuals with Autism Spectrum Disorder. Your support and engagement are invaluable, and I look forward to seeing the positive impact you will continue to make in the lives of those affected by ASD.